Detect and fend off gaslighting

How you can easily unmask gaslighting in partnership and at work using 11 signs and escape the manipulation trap in 5 steps

Anna-Lena Palek

CONTENT

What you can expect in this guide 1

What is Gaslighting? 4

Gaslighting - What does that even mean? 4

Consequences of Gaslighting 7

How does gaslighting work? 8

Excursus: The Stockholm Syndrome 10

How can I recognize gaslighting? 12

11 Signs of Gaslighting 12

Is a lie already gaslighting? 14

Typical Gaslighting Situations 15

In partnerships 16

At work 22

Gaslighting as a social phenomenon 25

Gaslighting in education 25

Gaslighting and narcissism 30

Gaslighting and sexism 32

Gaslighting and racism 35

Get out of the manipulation trap - How do I protect myself and others from gaslighting? 36

How can I protect myself? 36

In 5 steps out of the manipulation trap 39

How can I help those affected? 49

Where can I find professional help? 53

The game with shadows 55

What you can expect in this guide

Have you ever had the experience of being manipulated by a person to such an extent that you felt something was wrong with your perception? That you finally started to doubt your perceptive faculty, even your mental health? That you began to lose confidence in your senses because you were regularly told that you were perceiving reality incorrectly? You are not alone: this widespread phenomenon is called *gaslighting* and is a subtle, yet severe form of psychological violence that can have lasting effects on the victim's self-esteem.

"I never said that. You're just imagining it."
"It never happened that way."
"You're overreacting."
"You're crazy. You should get help."

These are just a few examples of phrases that are commonly used in gaslighting - if they sound familiar to you and, furthermore, you are no longer sure that you can still rely on your perception, you could possibly be affected.

Gaslighting can happen to us in different areas of life: in friendships and relationships, in the workplace, in political and sectarian structures - but in each case, this manipulative technique aims to make the victim doubt their perception and sanity in order to gain control and exercise power. But there are ways and means by which this destructive pattern can be seen through and broken!

In this guide, you will not only learn what exactly gaslighting actually is and how this mechanism works, but also how you can free yourself - and others - from the manipulation trap and ultimately emerge stronger from this crisis.

Important note on gender: For the sake of better readability, the generic masculine is used throughout this guide. It goes without saying, however, that in all cases members of all genders are addressed equally.

What is Gas-lighting?

GASLIGHTING - WHAT DOES THAT EVEN MEAN?

Over and over again, you hear and read about this term - gaslighting. It pops up in forums, blogs, newspaper reports and guidebooks, in the context of mental health in the workplace as well as in connection with parenting methods, narcissistic personality structures and toxic relationships. But what exactly is behind this word? And what is this name all about?

The term is based on the title of the play *Gas Light* by British playwright Patrick Hamilton. With the publication of the play in 1938, this phenomenon was addressed for the first time. The plot revolves around a married couple in which the husband is secretly searching for the jewels of a deceased tenant in the house they share. While he lights the gas lamps on the upper floor of the house during his search, the lamps in the rest of the house dim, but he vehemently denies this when his wife calls him on it. Over time, the man is able to convince his wife more and more that she is imagining the flickering lights, as well as the unfamiliar noises that reach her when he goes back to the attic. In order to support his lies, he gradually extends them to more and more areas of life and finally even makes her believe that her mother - like her - has gone crazy and died in a sanatorium.

When the film The *House of Lady Alquist,* based on the play *Gas Light,* appeared in 1944 and quickly gained popularity, the subject finally became common knowledge. But unfortunately, the sphere of influence of the phenomenon underlying the two aforementioned dramas is not limited to the fictional space of screenplays and theater scripts. Whether in partnerships or at the workplace, this particular form of manipulation comes to light again and again, in which the victim is made to believe that something is wrong with his or her perception. Political regimes or cults may also take advantage of this practice to gain control over the minds of their followers. In many cases of child sexual abuse, gaslighting is used to cloud memories of the experience and create emotional dependencies. However, gaslighting also repeatedly affects individual population groups or minorities in society as a whole - for example, it can also be found in the manifestation of racist and sexist structures.

The perfidious aspect of this manipulative tactic is that doubts are regularly sown in the victim (*Gaslightee*) about his or her own ability to perceive things on the basis of a relationship of trust over a longer period of time. In most cases, this process will have a lasting effect on the affected person's self-esteem and leave damage, the consequences of which the victim will often have to deal with for years to come. However, the perpetrator (*gaslighter*) is not always aware of his manipulative behavior. In particular, gaslighting can occur more frequently in certain clinical pictures, such as narcissism or sociopathy, without the gaslighter being aware of the toxic effects of their behavior.

CONSEQUENCES OF GAS-LIGHTING

Gaslighting acts like a creeping poison that slowly but surely attacks and breaks down the affected person's self-confidence. The feeling that one can no longer rely on one's own perception creates insecurity that gradually extends to all areas of life. As many Gaslightees develop the fear that they may have gone mad, they withdraw from their social life and try to cope with the situation alone.

The more the problem continues, the more drastic the consequences become - depression, anxiety, paranoia and feelings of alienation can occur. If these patterns are not recognized and broken in time, lasting psychological damage can result - in particular, people who were affected by gaslighting in childhood often struggle with the serious consequences throughout their lives and are often at risk of falling back into such relationships as adults.

HOW DOES GASLIGHTING WORK?

A basic prerequisite for gaslighting is that a relationship of trust exists between the perpetrator and the victim. Only on this basis is it possible for the gaslighter to make the gaslightee believe, through his targeted manipulation, that he perceives reality in a distorted way and is imagining things. Thus, the Gaslightee's confidence in his own perception gradually diminishes and he often feels an increasing pressure to justify himself to the Gaslighter. But the more the Gaslightee tries to defend himself, the more dependent he becomes on the Gaslighter's reaction. All attempts to regain the Gaslighter's recognition turn into the opposite. A power imbalance develops.

Once this mechanism is set in motion, it is difficult to break through again. The Gaslightee feels an increased desire for security, which he seeks in the Gaslighter's portrayal of reality, which the Gaslighter can in turn exploit to sow further doubts. The less the Gaslightee feels that he can rely on his own perception, the stronger his dependence on the Gaslighter's portrayal of reality becomes. In many cases, the gaslightee's dwindling self-esteem and fear of having gone mad cause him or her to withdraw from social contacts outside the toxic gaslighting relationship - an effect with fatal consequences, since an exchange with outsiders or friends could often help to reinforce confidence in one's own vision. Not infrequently, however, the perpetrators in gaslighting relationships even go so far as to persuade their victims that the entire environment has long since recognized that they are crazy and are only pretending that everything is fine with them out of pity.

Increasingly, the Gaslighter gains control over the Gaslightee's thinking until, in the worst case, the Gaslightee finds himself completely unable to think clearly on his own and finally becomes completely dependent on the Gaslighter constantly telling him what is right and wrong.

EXCURSUS: THE STOCKHOLM SYNDROME

Stockholm syndrome describes a psychological pheno-menon in which victims (usually of kidnapping or hostage-taking) develop a positive relationship with their perpetrator - in some cases they even fall in love. Similar to gaslighting, the complete loss of all security ensures that the victim trustingly places himself in the hands of the perpetrator because he represents the only fixed point of reference in the new situation.

The term Stockholm syndrome originated from the taking of hostages during a bank robbery that occurred in Stockholm in 1973. Four of the employees were taken hostage. According to media reports, over the next five days, the hostages developed solidarity with their captors and, as a result, showed increasing hostility toward the police. Even after the hostage-taking ended, they did not show any negative feelings toward the hostage-takers; on the contrary, they were even grateful to them for being released. Moreover, the hostages asked for mercy for the perpetrators and even visited them in prison. Similar to gaslighting, victims begin to identify and show solidarity with the perpetrators. By forming a positive attachment to the perpetrators, they create a sense of security. If they were to admit to themselves what is really going on, this perceived security would dissipate. Thus, the phenomenon described, like gaslighting, represents a protective mechanism of the soul that attempts to ensure the basic human need for attachment and security.

Stockholm syndrome differs from gaslighting, however, in that the former can be developed by the victim without deliberate influence by the perpetrator, whereas gaslighting necessarily requires conscious or unconscious, but in any case active, manipulation by the perpetrator. Nevertheless, these two phenomena not infrequently go hand in hand.

How can I recognize gaslighting?

11 SIGNS OF GASLIGHTING

1. They develop self-doubt and feel increasingly insecure.

2. They become more and more critical of themselves and feel they can't do anything right.

3. Other people's opinions are becoming increasingly important to you. With every action, every statement, you start to wonder how you will be received and increasingly look for recognition from outside.
4. If something goes wrong, immediately look for the fault in yourself.

5. The Gaslighter tells you what to think and feel. If you contradict him, he claims you are wrong/overreacting/being too sensitive or the like.

6. The Gaslighter seems to know exactly what those around you think about you ("We're all wondering what's wrong with you," "We all agree you're exaggerating," or the like).

7. In many cases, gaslighters also attract people from their immediate environment (circle of friends, work environment ...) to their site.

8. The Gaslighter puts words into your mouth that never came from you, or he denies statements that you can clearly remember. He makes it seem as if the reason for this discrepancy lies with you and your supposedly distorted perception. In the end, you may no longer be sure yourself what was actually said/happened and what you are only imagining.
9. You feel pressured by the Gaslighter. This can happen through threats (e.g. "If you don't ..., then I'll have to ...") or by him giving you the cold shoulder as soon as you don't behave according to his idea.

10. When you express a feeling, especially a negative one, the Gaslighter lets you know you are wrong about your feeling.

11. You start to believe the assessment of others more than your own feeling.

IS A LIE ALREADY GASLIGHTING?

But what is the difference between a "conventional" lie and gaslighting? Where is the dividing line between the two? Or is every untruth already a form of manipulation that could be called gaslighting?

It is certainly not easy to clearly distinguish between the two in every situation, and the transitions can sometimes be fluid. In principle, however, the following applies: An untruth that does not explicitly question the other person's ability to perceive is a lie (and therefore naturally not okay), but not yet gaslighting. Only if your counterpart expresses in the course of this also that there is something wrong with your perception, one speaks of gaslighting. In the following chapter, you will find some examples that clearly show the difference.

Typical Gaslighting Situations

The following chapter presents some situations in which exemplary gaslighting behavior can be identified. Of course, gaslighting can occur in countless constellations with diverse motives, but in order to provide certain real-life clues, some common patterns are shown here. All constellations shown are fictitious, but based on true events.

IN PARTNERSHIPS

Gaslighting often occurs in the context of the issue around fidelity and infidelity. Both the jealous and the unfaithful person can become the gaslighter. For example, when covering up affairs, the gaslightee is often persuaded that he or she is imagining the signs that might indicate infidelity.

Markus and Lina have been a couple for more than 10 years and married for 3 years. Markus works as an architect, Lina is an actress and often travels for longer periods due to guest acting engagements. Once, having just returned from a trip, she discovers a long black hair on the sofa. Lina herself has blond hair and there is no one with such hair in their mutual circle of friends. However, she knows that in Markus in his architectural office has a colleague with long black hair. Despite initial inhibitions - after all, she doesn't want to appear controlling - she cautiously approaches Markus about it. He reacts irritably. "I told you that my colleague was here the day before yesterday because we had to continue working on our joint project!" Lina is surprised - she can't remember Markus talking about it, even though she had spoken to him on the phone yesterday. Not even the information that the two of them are working on a project together sounds familiar to her. Unsettled, she remarks both things, whereupon Markus replies increasingly irritated: "Of course you knew about it! I've told you several times. But when you're on tour, you have nothing else on your mind but your theater stuff. No wonder you always forget everything." He then leaves the room in a huff. Lina's uncertainty grows. Has she really forgotten? Or overheard? Is she acting selfishly without realizing it? Does she take herself and her work too seriously and lose sight of her fellow human beings? Does Markus feel set back by her? Feelings of guilt germinate in her ...

Lina has obviously caught Markus. To save face, he doesn't deny the lady's visit - which would hardly be a believable lie in view of the hair lying around - but pretends to have told Lina about the visit. But that's not all: to further unsettle her and make her feel that *she* has in fact made a mistake and is now in Markus's debt, he attacks her on a personal level by insinuating that she is less interested in him than in herself and that she is neglecting the relationship because of her art.

But the reverse case also exists: For example, a jealous Gaslighter will accuse the Gaslightee of infidelity at every opportunity, dragging circumstantial evidence for it by the hair and conveying to the Gaslightee, even in everyday situations, that it is behaving impiously.

Verena and Stefan have only known each other for a few months and are very happily in love with each other. It's New Year's Eve and the couple is invited to friends of Verena's to celebrate the turn of the year in a fitting manner. In a boisterous celebratory mood, the two arrive at the party and very soon start talking to various people there. By chance, Stefan also meets a former fellow student among the guests and begins a long conversation with her - after all, they haven't seen each other since the weightless years of their studies and now have a lot to exchange.

On the way home, Verena is silent. Stefan gradually notices that she is behaving differently than usual, but can't make sense of it - after all, they had a nice evening? After a few minutes, Stefan breaks the silence and cautiously asks Verena if everything is all right. "Of course," she returns icily. "I just don't want to bother you - after all, you obviously enjoyed the evening. So my presence is certainly rather inconvenient for you ..." Stefan no longer understands the world. Has he done something wrong?

What is it with Verena? Did it bother her that he was talking to his old girlfriend? Stefan tries to take her hand, but she pulls it away. "Oh, don't force yourself to do anything. It's obvious that you would much rather have taken this other one home with you! I suppose I'm supposed to be the cheap substitute now?" - Stefan can't believe his ears. Verena is actually jealous! Does she really think he would prefer the old girlfriend to her? Just because he had a longer conversation with her?

He rummages in his memory ... were there possibly situations in which the impression could have arisen? Did he get involved in a flirtation without realizing it? "I'm sorry, Verena, but you've got it all wrong!" says Stefan. "I know Laura from university, we had the same circle of friends back then and were often out together. But there was never anything more! After graduation, we lost track of each other and have just met again for the first time since then. Of course we had a lot to talk about, but that doesn't mean anything!" - "Oh, so it means nothing," Verena returns. "And the fact that you literally undressed her with your looks, in front of all the guests, that doesn't mean anything either? And that you pretended in front of her that we didn't even know each other?" Stefan shakes his head in irritation - what does Verena mean? He was simply talking to Laura, after all. And

Verena seemed to be having a great time all the time with her friends - it never occurred to him that she might be bored or feeling neglected.

He wants to defend himself, but doesn't quite know what to say ... without meaning to or even realizing it, he seems to have seriously hurt Verena. Yet he was only talking to an old friend! His thoughts begin to race. Has he possibly behaved inappropriately after all? "But Verena," he says. "That's not true at all! We were just talking! I didn't have any ulterior motives at all - and Laura certainly didn't either!" He had tried to soothe her, but his words missed their mark. She only became more irritated. "Surely it wasn't just me who noticed what was going on between you! My girlfriends could hardly believe that you were pulling something like this in front of me. I'm sorry, Stefan, but it was completely obvious. I hope I never have to experience something like that again, otherwise it'll be over with us faster than you can pronounce Laura's name."

In this case, Verena's jealousy conveys to her partner that he has behaved inappropriately. If Stefan were sure that there had been nothing reprehensible about his behavior, a development in the direction of gaslighting would be ruled out.

However, as he takes Verena's accusations to heart and questions his behavior, this mechanism kicks in. In retrospect, he examines the event for possible mistakes he might have made, develops feelings of guilt, and resolves to be more careful when talking to other women in the future. In all likelihood, he will be less impartial on the next occasion than he was on the evening in question. Whether Verena will be satisfied with that, however, is questionable. She will probably make him believe that he is betraying their relationship until he finally withdraws completely from all contact.

Of course, there are countless other contexts in couple relationships with which gaslighting can occur. On the Internet, there are several testimonials from those affected, as well as forums where former Gaslightees can exchange ideas and offer mutual support, e.g. https://gaslighting.org/, https://beziehung.gofeminin.de/forum/gaslighting-manipulation-fd1036060.

In everyday working life, too, situations occur time and again in which a person is told that his or her perception is faulty. Hierarchical power structures further encourage this process, as does the insecurity that can arise due to dependence on the job. The following example describes the story of a young journalist who experiences sexist gaslighting at work.

Theresa is a dedicated young woman who has recently started working as a journalist in the editorial department of a prestigious magazine. It is her dream job; she has fought hard for this position and approaches her work accordingly with self-sacrifice. The fact that she is the only woman in her department and that all her other colleagues are also at least ten years older than her and have already been working in the company for years is something she didn't think was a problem at first. But very soon it becomes apparent that this discrepancy leads to certain tensions: From her first day at work, Theresa feels her efforts are not sufficiently valued and she feels uncomfortable in this male-dominated environment. Her enthusiastic basic attitude becomes her undoing. Between the generally disapproving gestures of her colleagues, disparaging remarks and even occasional sexist remarks are mixed in now and then.

Despite her excellent qualifications, she is only ever assigned the least demanding jobs and has to perform tasks for which she would not be responsible in the slightest - she is even coerced into making coffee, even though she doesn't drink any herself. As Theresa becomes increasingly insecure, she cranks up her drive even further and goes about her work with even more commitment, but this does nothing to change the working atmosphere. Realizing this, the fall of Theresa's expectations to the ground only increases. So, contrary to her intentions, she slides further and further down this power gradient. When she talks to her colleagues about the fact that she doesn't feel valued, she only gets the answer "Don't be a jerk!" or "It's hard, this job!" as if her colleagues' behavior had nothing to do with her feelings. The head of department, too, meets her descriptions with incomprehension and embellishments, so that she increasingly gets the feeling that her perception could be distorted.

What happens to Theresa here is a widespread form of gaslighting. Her colleagues and superiors take advantage of her professionally more secure position to make her feel inferior. Since she is not only younger than her colleagues, but also the only woman in her company, sexism is additionally mixed into the general disrespect with which she is treated. When she openly addresses the problem, her criticism is rejected and she is accused of being oversensitive and unable to cope with the high demands of her job.

Gaslighting as a social phenomenon

GASLIGHTING IN EDUCATION

Emotional violence in parenting can manifest itself in many facets. Since children are absolutely dependent on their parents for their existence and must first learn the ability to form their own opinions, it is in the nature of things that they are particularly at risk of falling victim to manipulation, even gaslighting. Of course, in most cases this does not happen out of malicious intent on the part of the parents or educators, which unfortunately does not make the effects on the child's psyche any less serious.

It already starts on a small scale when parents or educators, out of insecurity or shame, resort to white

lies with which they want to cover up what has happened - an example: A single mother promises her
child that she will take him to the zoo on the weekend.
At short notice, however, she is offered a well-paid job
by her employer, which would be a real boon in her
current financial predicament. Of course she has
scruples - the child is already looking forward to the
zoo visit so much and has been talking about nothing
else for days, she doesn't want to spoil this joy for him.
On the other hand, she can hardly refuse this order in
her situation, especially since she fears that if she refu-
ses, she will be passed over for future job offers as well.

Plagued by remorse, she accepts the assignment,
but doesn't tell her child about the change of plans, in
the groundless hope that the child might not notice
that the weekend is passing without a visit to the zoo.
But when the weekend arrives, the child is jumping up
and down excitedly in the apartment early in the mor-
ning, asking every minute when they are finally
leaving. The mother feels cornered. How is she supposed to explain this to her child now? So instead of telling the child the unpleasant truth, she tries to deny
the promise and says, "I said *maybe* we'd go to the zoo,"
which is of course met with loud protest. She continues, "I can't go anywhere with you anyway, the way

you're acting. Otherwise they'll keep you in the monkey house right away." Thus, the mother has cleverly gotten out of the affair. But at the same time, she has not only lied to her child, she has also conveyed to him that he has misremembered something and that, in addition, his behavior is to blame for the fact that the much longed-for excursion cannot take place. In many families such situations occur sporadically. Certainly, it is important to avoid such situations if possible and to strive for open communication instead, but a one-time occurrence of this phenomenon will not yet leave a lasting mark on the child's soul.

But unfortunately, much more serious cases also occur, in which children are almost systematically manipulated by their parents or educators throughout childhood. Especially in cases of physical violence and sexual abuse, extreme cases of gaslighting often play a decisive role. For example, the child concerned is often persuaded that he or she has not experienced any beatings, assaults, rapes, etc., but is only imagining them; or worse still, the child is made to believe that he or she is making up these stories in order to torment his or her "poor" parents.

This creates a deep gap between what the child perceives itself and what it is prescribed to perceive.

Not only due to the still incompletely developed judgment, but also due to the emotional and existential dependence of the child on the caregiver, it is forced into an ambivalent position. In order to be able to maintain the necessary trusting bond, the affected children begin to place the blame on themselves. They develop the feeling that something is wrong with them and that they are "bad" children under whose tyranny the pitiful (infallible) adults have to suffer. It becomes especially bad when the parents begin to involve the child's friends in the web of manipulation, for example, by telling them or their parents how difficult the child is, that he steals, lies, or the like, and that one must be careful of him. Listed below are some phrases that are common in gaslighting relationships between parents and children. If some of these sound familiar from your own past, it is quite possible that you were also affected by them in childhood.

- "Are you saying your mom/dad is lying?"
- "I never said that."
- "I never did."
- "You're lying through your teeth."
- "Don't talk nonsense."
- "It can't be."

- "It hurts me much more than it hurts you." (punishments, beatings, etc.)
- "You brought this on yourself."
- "Don't be like that."
- "You're making a mountain out of a molehill again."
- "Every time it's nice, you have to break everything."
- "You have no sense of humor."
- "There's something wrong with you."
- "You belong in an insane asylum, don't you?"
- "You don't know how good you have it."
- "The others will also realize what a terrible child you really are."

Parents who treat their children in this way often have a narcissistic personality disorder, which is not always recognized as such. Very often, these harmful experiences also take place in secret, without outsiders such as friends, teachers or neighbors even noticing. If a child affected by gaslighting does show behavior that suggests something is wrong, parents often smile it off and downplay it as a normal childish whim.

Whether out of misplaced politeness, disinterest or actual ignorance on the part of the environment - far too seldom is anything done after such situations to at least find out whether there might not be emotional abuse in the domestic environment. And at the same time, the mechanisms of gaslighting work so subtly that it is often difficult for outsiders to assess whether and to what extent there is abuse of the child. However, the effects on the child's soul are serious in any case and usually irreversible or can only be brought under control through years of therapy and painful reappraisal processes. The feeling of being defective, disturbed in perception and generally guilty, anchored from childhood, nests and has a lasting effect on the affected person's self-confidence and attachment behavior. Often, individuals who were affected by Gaslighting in childhood continue to enter into relationships as adults in which the destructive pattern is repeated. They have learned that relationship means manipulation.

GASLIGHTING AND NARCISSISM

Gaslighting is also frequently experienced when dealing with narcissists. They are often not even aware of how damaging their behavior can be for the soul of their counterpart.

Since they put their own well-being above

everything else, they often lack empathy and tend to perceive their fellow human beings as a reflecting surface on which they can experience themselves. In this context, their fellow human beings are supposed to serve them primarily in order to satisfy their needs or as a means to an end so that they can achieve their goals. However, since narcissists can often display a very self-confident and charming demeanor that does not make them recognizable as narcissists at first glance, it is also easy for them to win over their fellow human beings at first. This is why it is not uncommon to find them in highly placed professional positions or political offices. However, the self-confidence of narcissists is fragile and they need the feeling of being able to exercise control. Individuals with narcissistic personality disorder will use any means to achieve this, as long as it results in getting what they want. When they realize that they do not have "enough" power over their counterpart, they often try to make them feel insecure and weaken their self-esteem. This allows them to perceive themselves as the "stronger" one.

Admitting mistakes is usually difficult for people with a narcissistic personality structure, which is why they often portray events afterwards as if only others were responsible for all misfortunes or injustices.

Often they even portray themselves as victims and thus attract additional pity. They can convince not only others but also themselves of their distorted version of reality so convincingly that they eventually believe it themselves. Especially when gaslighters themselves are convinced of their distorted facts, there is a danger that the manipulation will continue and that those involved will be pushed further and further into their positions.

GASLIGHTING AND SEXISM

At the latest since the MeToo debate made waves in October 2017, the topic of sexism has increasingly become the focus of public perception and, in the course of this, the associated communication schemes.

A closer look quickly reveals that many of the principles inherent in gaslighting can also be found in sexist structures. For example, countless women who have experienced a sexual assault experience that a *victim-blaming process* takes place afterwards. Affected women repeatedly report that police officers, family members or friends do not believe their accounts and shift the blame back onto the victim. As if this could justify the crime, the women concerned are asked, for example, how they were dressed at the time of the crime, where and at what time they were, whether they were alone, whether they had drunk alcohol, etc. In this way, they are indirectly or directly accused of having committed the crime. In this way, they are indirectly or directly accused of having provoked the perpetrator to commit an assault through their appearance or behavior. The perpetrator is thus excused and the victim is made responsible for what happened - this is doubly perfidious in that the victim not only has to live with the serious consequences of the sexual abuse, but also has to cope with feelings of guilt. "What should I have done differently so that I wouldn't have had to experience this?" is a question that victims often ask themselves - and with this, the first step of gaslighting has already taken place: The victim was made to feel that it was his or her own fault that something was done to him or her.

"Now don't be like that yet!" "They're just harmless niceties." "Don't be so uptight!" - girls and women who want to defend themselves against unwanted advances are regularly confronted with statements like these. Whether in the family circle, at work, or in public, almost every woman encounters such a situation - and thus gaslighting - at least once in her life. In these examples, it is suggested to the affected person that what she is bothered about is completely legitimate and that she perceives a problem where there is none - with the logical conclusion that the problem lies in her perception.

It is an incontrovertible fact that every person should be allowed to set his or her own limits, both psychological and physical, and that these must be accepted by all fellow human beings without fail. However, by ignoring and undermining this fact, those affected gradually lose this security (or they grow up without an awareness of it from the outset). Sexual abuse of children and domestic violence also often entail gaslighting based on the above statements, or even denial of what happened: "It never happened that way."

GASLIGHTING AND RACISM

Structural racism is another issue that has finally become a topic of public discussion in recent years - the May 25, 2020 murder of African American George Floyd was another major contributing factor.

But as much as voices are raised on one side demanding the recognition and abolition of racist structures, opposing voices also speak up, not only trying to justify these structures, but even denying their existence. "There is certainly no racism behind this, it was just a coincidence/pitch," is a common reaction when criticizing injustices behind which a racist attitude is suspected. The people affected arc given the feeling that they are misperceiving things, imagining connections and that the problem really lies with them. Statements such as "I don't see any skin colors," "Racism doesn't exist anymore," etc. deny this structural problem and the experiences of the countless people affected are declared null and void.

Get out of the manipulation trap - How do I protect myself and others from gaslighting?

HOW CAN I PROTECT MYSELF?

Manipulative behavior and gaslighting can affect anyone. Falling victim to it is not a sign of weakness or even stupidity! There are some things you can do and observe to prevent yourself from becoming the target of a gaslighting attack. If you are sensitized to these patterns and already their subtlest signs, you will recognize even the most devious attempts to manipulate you as such and let them bounce off you ineffectively. A basic prerequisite for this is, of course, that you are aware of the danger posed by gaslighting and are well informed about how it works, its signs and consequences. In this way, you can differentiate exactly when questionable patterns occur and take further action immediately against this background.

First and foremost: Let your heart be your compass! Listen to your feelings - because they give you the most reliable information about how you are doing. But even people who have no experience of how it feels when their own feelings are questioned may find it difficult at first to listen uncompromisingly and unconditionally in search of an answer to the question: How am I actually doing? After all, society's standard assumes that in the course of our lives we learn not to be overly influenced by our feelings and to place our ability to think rationally above any sensitivity. But does this really help us to develop a healthy and happy approach to ourselves and our fellow human beings? Don't we often base our actions on reason, doing or not doing something just because we think it should be done? Don't we often make decisions after careful consideration, but ignore the voice of our gut feeling?

In all situations in life, we intuitively recognize whether we feel good or not. The reasons for our respective feeling may be partially still so hazy to us, nevertheless the feeling is undeniably present and has to communicate something to us. Whether we feel spontaneously attracted to someone or suddenly the alarming feeling arises in us that something is not right: it is worthwhile to take this into account. In this way, your inner voice can warn you early on if you are forming a bond with someone who will turn out to be harmful to you in retrospect. The stronger a person's self-confidence is, the less chance gaslighters have of making a difference with their perfidious game.

IN 5 STEPS OUT OF THE MANI-PULATION TRAP

Now that a number of examples have been listed and their signs and consequences explained, the question arises: What should be done if one suspects oneself of being a victim of gaslighting or that someone in one's own environment could be affected? What steps are necessary to sort out the increasing self-doubt and re-gain ground or help other people out of their situation? Here you will find a detailed guide with concrete as-sistance. The next chapter will go into more detail about how you can assist others affected on their way out of a gaslighting relationship.

1. get clarity

Whether at work, in a relationship or in family struc-tures - be on your guard if you increasingly get the im-pression that something is wrong with your percep-tion. Before you let yourself become too unsettled, cre-ate a clear picture of your situation. This may sound paradoxical in view of the situation, but it is neverthel-ess possible to a certain extent. Namely, by doing exactly what the potential gaslighter probably wants to keep you from doing: Trusting your gut. If you don't

feel comfortable in your current situation or think something is wrong, take it seriously and get to the bottom of it.

To do this, switch off the distinction between true
and false for a moment and formulate for yourself as
precisely as possible what makes you feel insecure
about the current situation, how you feel, what fears
you have, etc. Ideally, you should also make compari-
sons (if possible) with earlier times when you did not
know this person. Ignore nascent thoughts such as
"But I'm just imagining things" - the main thing here is
how you feel and how you perceive things. So don't be
afraid to take stock honestly.

2. keep a diary

It is recommended that you also put the thought processes just mentioned down on paper. If you have
everything in black and white, it will be easier for you
to organize your thoughts. It is best to make it a habit
to document your emotional state as precisely as possible every day. It is also particularly helpful in recog-
nizing gaslighting structures to take paper and pen directly after all conversations with the gaslighter in order to record what was said as verbatim as possible or
to communicate with the person only in writing, e.g.

by e-mail or text message (which is of course more feasible with work colleagues or superiors than with close friends or members of your own household). This way, you always have the option of accessing the content of conversations that took place further back in time without it being distorted by the memory.

In addition, you can factually refute any claims made by the other party by comparing them with your own notes. Another advantage of writing this down is that later, when you find yourself talking to outsiders, you have a tangible piece of evidence for the complications at hand, which can be of particular interest if higher authorities have to be involved, for example the youth welfare office in the context of a separation or the works council in the case of gaslighting at the workplace.

3. seek exchange with other people

As already explained, the relationship of trust between Gaslighter and Gaslightee is like a breeding ground on which the manipulations can flourish. However, this process can only proceed truly undisturbed if the influences from outside this relationship remain as small as possible. Any objective opinion from outsiders can therefore shake the gaslighter's construct, which is why the gaslighter will try to discredit the environment in some way as early as possible. This can be done in many ways: For example, by transferring his own views to the environment ("We all agree that you are exaggerating") or by impressing upon the gaslightee that the others are only pretending that everything is fine out of pity.

If the gaslighter manages to sufficiently weaken the external influences in time, the fruits of his intrigues can flourish completely unchecked. In order to prevent exactly this, you should seek exchange with other people in any case. In this way, you can carry out *reality checks for* yourself at an early stage in order to be able to weigh up whether the gaslighter's statements are justified.

First and foremost, consult friends with whom you have a stable relationship of trust, but who are nevertheless involved as little as possible in the relationship between you and the gaslighter. This will help assure you that the person has a largely objective view of the situation. Also, use your notes - these will also help you remain objective and consistent.

In addition to exchanging information with outsiders, it can also be helpful to contact people who are also affected. Especially in the case of suspected gaslighting at work or in the family, it makes sense to talk openly with others involved about any attempts at manipulation. On the one hand, this may reveal that some people have already found a way to deal with it; on the other hand, your initiative may make individuals aware of their situation in the first place!

However, it can also happen that neither by talking to outsiders nor to involved persons do you reach insights that are conclusive for you. Or that even after the exchange with all these instances, the feeling remains that there is something wrong with you and your perception. If this is the case, you should definitely seek professional help at this point. A first step may be to pick up the phone: The help hotline for women (08000 116 016), for example, provides advice and information around the clock. If it is a case of gaslighting at your workplace, contact the works council. Under the heading "Where can I find professional help?" at the end of the guide, you will find other points of contact where you can get acute help or long-term psychological support.

You may also want to confront the gaslighter yourself. However, this is only advisable if you feel strong enough to expose yourself to this stressful situation. In addition, confronting the Gaslighter is only useful in a few cases at all. For example, if you are dealing with a person with narcissistic personality disorder, it is not advisable to talk to them, as it would most likely only wear you down even more and no improvement could be expected from it.

If you nevertheless come to the conclusion that a clarifying conversation with the gaslighter might be appropriate in your case and you feel able to do so, prepare yourself well for it. This is because it is very likely that in the course of the conversation your counterpart will try even harder than usual to make you uncomfortable. And even if the person is close to you: Don't let yourself be put off by any cross shots. You are sufficiently aware of what bothers you about the other person's behavior and you have also exchanged views with outsiders, so it is your right to communicate your demands.

Be aware that a conversation with the gaslighter is only productive if the gaslighter is willing to listen to you and take you seriously. If you notice in the course of the conversation that you are getting nothing but resistance and that no attention is being paid to you, break off the conversation. It would be pointless to continue here, as improvement is only possible if there is sufficient willingness to listen and cooperate.

In the lucky event that you get through to the person in question and he or she is willing to change his or her behavior, you can work together to find a way out of the situation. Ideally, you should seek professional help on both sides, because it may also be in the gaslighter's best interest that such disagreements do not occur again in the future.

Unfortunately, however, in most cases a clarifying conversation is either ruled out from the outset or does not achieve the desired improvement in the situation - if it does not even make the situation worse. Therefore, it is usually necessary to take further steps.

4. break the contact

The deeper you have already been drawn into the gaslighting vortex, the more difficult it will be to fight your way back to the surface. If you have successfully carried out the steps up to this point, break off the gaslighter contact with immediate effect if possible - or at least reduce it to such an extent that you can gain a certain distance from the situation.

If the person in question is merely a distant friend or work colleague, it is naturally easier to distance yourself completely than with a family member or partner. But even if the person in question is close to you, realize for a moment what is going on here: the manipulation creates an emotional dependency that puts the relationship with each other into an enormous imbalance.

Humans are fundamentally very adaptable, which is why it is very likely that over time you will have become accustomed to the many restrictions and harassments and will no longer even perceive them as such. Subjectively, this mechanism does reduce the damage caused; however, it does not detract from the seriousness of the situation. Therefore, ask yourself the question: Do you really want to live in a relationship that permanently raises self-doubt in you and puts a lasting psychological strain on you?

If you are afraid that your partner might get physical with you, force you to stay with him or her against your will, or otherwise assault you, be sure to consult the help hotline (08000 116 016) or a similar hotline. There you can also get information on victim protection as well as contact to support facilities in your area. Psychological violence is in no way less devastating than physical violence and, moreover, is equally punishable. So do not hesitate to get help.

5. silence your inner gaslighter

Gaslighting inevitably leaves its mark on the person affected. Many of the possible consequential damages have already been mentioned; apart from a generally weakened self-esteem, the accusations and insinuations on the part of the Gaslighter have often already burned themselves in so strongly that the Gaslightee still has to struggle with recurring thought and feeling patterns established by Gaslighting even after this grueling relationship has been resolved.

Just as the way our parents treat us in childhood is internalized and makes itself heard again throughout life as an inner voice, the psyche also subconsciously internalizes the voice of the gaslighter. Feelings of insecurity, worthlessness or alienation associated with gaslighting can therefore persist long after the toxic contact has been broken off - the poison continues to have an effect. To counteract this, it is advisable to seek long-term psychological help.

It may be that you suddenly feel better and freer directly after the detachment from the gaslighting relationship (the separation, the break-off of contact, etc.). This is all too logical; after all, you have lived under the dictates of the harmful influence for a considerable time and can now finally think and act for yourself again.

But be aware that this initial euphoric state should not be taken as proof that you have completely overcome the episode. Every learning process takes time and rarely does a healing process proceed in a linear fashion - it is quite normal if, after an initial flight of fancy, you feel thrown back again and have the impression that you can no longer get any further.

HOW CAN I HELP THOSE AFFECTED?

Whether at work, among friends, or in relation to sexist or racist structures - if you perceive gaslighting in your environment or even suspect it, do not remain inactive! Gaslighting is anything but harmless and can have lasting psychological consequences. Often, people affected by gaslighting develop depression or anxiety disorders. So if you even suspect someone in your circle might be affected: Keep your eyes open and, if possible, try to stand by the affected person. Of course, professional help should be sought, especially in severe cases, but it can make it significantly easier for those affected to find a way out of the gaslighting relationship if they receive assistance and support from those around them.

Especially if the Gaslighting process is quite advanced and the Gaslightee has already lost large parts of his self-confidence and trust in his self-awareness, it is invaluable to signal to him that you stand by him, that you believe him, and that he can trust you without hesitation. You can help a Gaslightee with these concrete steps:

1. Observe the situation!

As soon as you even suspect that someone in your environment might be affected by gaslighting, keep a discreet eye on the situation. Gaslighting often works by subtle means that are not apparent at first glance. However, if you suspect that this problem could be present in your professional or private environment, try to gain more clarity about it. A one-time situation is not necessarily decisive, but if the indications accumulate, your alarm bells should ring in any case! If your suspicions are confirmed, act immediately to help the person concerned!

2. Talk to the person concerned!

This may not always be easy - especially if you do not have a close relationship of trust with the person. But who knows what a great service you will be doing them!

Gaslightees themselves are often unaware of the perfidious game they are involved in - if a suspicion to this effect should occasionally arise in them, they usually do not trust this suspicion themselves. In this case, it can be helpful to be encouraged by an outsider. But caution is required here - of course, this is a highly sensitive topic! Not only because gaslightees can quickly get the impression that you want to patronize them or imply weakness, but also because gaslightees are often unsure who they can still trust and who they can't - especially if they have been told by their tormentor that the whole environment has already recognized how crazy the person is. So always consider the emotional situation of the Gaslightee and treat him as you would like to be treated in a similar situation.

3. Listen. Be there.

Once the Gaslightee has come to trust you, you will probably play an important role for him. Not least because a Gaslighting relationship - toxic as it may be - is based on a strong bond and mutual dependence. If the Gaslightee recognizes these patterns and starts to break away from them, he will also lose a lot of supposed stability and security. Very likely, he will then first seek this from you.

Of course, you can and should only grant this to a certain extent, even in very close friendships. Therefore, it is all the more important to also seek the professional help of a psychological counseling center or a psychotherapist. Nevertheless, with your open ears, you can make an important contribution to the Gaslightee feeling grounded again.

4. Keep your own boundaries!

However, the fact that you are there for the Gaslightee should in no way mean that you have to accept everything without contradiction. You should listen to him without bias, but you do not have to tell him what he wants to hear if you perceive something differently than he does.

A dialogue conducted from different points of view is an important sign of mutual respect and it will even strengthen the Gaslightee in his process if he experiences that you can definitely be of divided opinion without starting a power struggle about it. In the same way you should not let yourself be taken over and be available to him beyond your own strength at any time of the day or night! You can accompany him, but you should not carry him.

5. Put the gaslightee professional help!

Especially after a protracted gaslighting relationship that has left serious damage in its wake, it is absolutely necessary to consult a psychological counseling center or therapy. There are often inhibitions about taking this step, but you can make it easier for the person to get started by, for example, offering to help find a therapist or checking in regularly to see how they are doing in their search. Signal that seeking help is not a sign of weakness and show interest in how things are going!

WHERE CAN I FIND PROFESSIO-NAL HELP?

If gaslighting takes place in the work environment, a first step can be to turn to superiors, provided of course that they are not themselves involved. In some companies and universities, there is also the possibility of contacting women's or equal opportunity officers. Often, they can also provide addresses that can be contacted for further therapeutic treatment.

Of course, it is also possible to look for a suitable therapist on your own. The Internet even offers search engines where you can search specifically for someone who meets your needs by setting various filters (e.g. www.therapie.de, Kassenärztliche Bundesvereinigung). Alternatively, you can contact psychological counseling centers such as ProFamilia. These are also offered by some church organizations (e.g. Diakonie).

For acute help, you can also contact a telephone counselling service. These are usually available throughout and are free of charge.

Telephone counselling of the
Protestant Church: 0800 / 111 0 111
and Catholic Church: 0800 / 111 0 222

Of course, you can take the help of both numbers regardless of your religion or denomination.

More information: www.telefonseelsorge.de

The game with shadows

Although the term gaslighting and public awareness of this mechanism are not even a hundred years old, the issue itself is probably as old as humanity itself. Research into this field is also still largely in its infancy, but as public awareness grows, so do attempts by psychologists and journalists to get to the bottom of this issue and how it works.

Through this guidebook, you received a first overview of all the mechanisms inherent in the gas lighting and their effects; but also assistance that can help you on the way out of the gaslighting trap. Getting out of this complicated situation requires a lot of strength and can be very painful; but once this crisis is over, you will feel better and go about your further life with a completely new self-confidence.

Finally, I would like to give you some further literature tips:

> • Julia Naue: *When Others Manipulate Our Perception.*
>
> • Sandra Berthaler: *Psycho-Terror in Relationships: Manipulation to the point of insanity: This is how "gaslighters" abuse their victims.*
>
> • *Gaslighting is subtle psychological abuse - It is often close people who torment their victims through this kind of manipulation. A field report.*
>
> • Henrike Möller: *Gaslighting: When Perception is Controlled by Others.*
>
> • Kira Cossa: *Daughters of Narcissistic Mothers: Gaslighting.*
>
> • *Strategy "Gaslighting": How deliberate manipulation of reality makes people sick.*
>
> • Bärbel Wardetzki: *Gaslighting: The Complete Insecurity - "I Thought I Was Going Crazy".*
>
> • Verena Maria Dittrich: *Gaslighting: The Perfidious Pleasure of* Manipulation
>
> • Jan Drees: *On emotional abuse,*
>
> • Gaslighting - Subtle Psychological Abuse |

Kleinerdrei

- Jan Drees: *Gaslighting: I'm afraid of my ex - about the feature*
- The Chicks: "Gaslighter"